Bloom's Modern Critical Views

JOSÉ SARAMAGO

Edited and with an introduction by
Harold Bloom
Sterling Professor of the Humanities
Yale University

CHELSEA HOUSE
PUBLISHERS
A Haights Cross Communications ✦ Company®
Philadelphia

Library of Congress Cataloging-in-Publication Data

José Saramago / [edited by] Harold Bloom.
    p. cm. — (Bloom's modern critical views)
  Includes bibliographical references and index.
  ISBN 0-7910-8133-8 (alk. paper)
  1. Saramago, José—Criticism and interpretation. I. Bloom, Harold. II. Series.
PQ9281.A66Z73 2004
869.3'42—dc22
                                    2004024078

Contributing Editor: Pamela Loos

Cover designed by Keith Trego

Cover photo: European Press Photo Agency, EFE/Toni Albir

Layout by EJB Publishing Services

Editor's Note

My Introduction covers Saramago's work from *Baltasar and Blimunda* on through *All the Names*, stressing his extraordinary variety, his refusal to repeat himself.

Richard Preto-Rodas praises the high irony of *Baltsar and Blimunda*, while Mary L. Daniel probes the labyrinthine symbolism of *The Stone Raft*.

Two of Saramago's plays are studied by Gene Stevens Forrest as Marxist reinterpretations of history, after which Giovanni Pontiero capably confronts *The Year of the Death of Ricardo Reis*.

David Frier examines Saramago's novels as assaults upon the Catholic Church, and as goads to the popular sense of freedom, after which I analyze *The Gospel According to Jesus Christ*, which I judge to be Saramago's masterpiece.

The Stone Raft returns in Mark Sabine's reading as an attack upon the European Union, while Ron Sousa meditates upon *The History of the Siege of Lisbon*, another sublime Saramago revision of conventional history.

Paulo de Mediaro finds in Saramago's "travel book", *Journey to Portugal*, further instances of the sly revisionism of this subtly subversive artist, after which Andrew Laird concludes our volume with a consideration of Saramago's *The Cave*, a startling reimagining of Plato's most famous myth.

HAROLD BLOOM

Introduction

Rereading Saramago, I always feel like Ulysses trying to keep my hold on Proteus, the metamorphic god of ocean; he keeps slipping away. From *Baltasar and Blimunda* on through *The Cave*, Saramago is in constant change, not merely from fiction to fiction, but within each work. I don't know the genre of any of his books, except his masterpiece (in my view), *The Gospel According to Jesus Christ*, as that I suppose has to be called a gospel, though it brings very bad news indeed: a Jesus betrayed by God the Father; a Satan who is a mild bystander, really a good shepherd, and so named Pastor; a God so self-indulgent that he sacrifices Jesus solely in order to extend his worshippers from the small elite of the Jews, to a myriad of Christians. There is also this God's evident, sadistic relish in sacrificing not only Jesus but a vast array of subsequent martyrs, all tortured to death or executed by an exuberant panoply of ingenious devices.

But I have considered Saramago's *Gospel* elsewhere, and shall revisit it later only in passing. Here I begin with the outrageous and delicious *Baltasar and Blimunda* (1987), though to characterize any single narrative by Saramago as being more deliciously outrageous than the others is a disputable judgment.

T.S. Eliot was fond of describing himself as Anglo-Catholic, Royalist, and classicist. He could have added anti-Semite, and I have always wondered how he would have reacted had Great Britain been successfully invaded and occupied by the Nazis? I don't know that Saramago needs to describe himself at all: he is certainly neither Catholic nor Royalist, and he is too diverse and inventive for any stance like classicist to subsume him. Like Jorge Luis Borges, Saramago is a free man, and his books exalt freedom, generally by depicting its dreadful alternatives. *Baltasar and Blimunda* is Saramago's historical romance, set in the frightening Portugal of the early eighteenth century, a country where the Enlightenment had not yet arrived. Public entertainment still was constituted by acts of faith, in which heretics, Jews, and everyone else who offended either Church or King were burned alive, to the edification of the true believers.

These fires burn throughout the book, but most dreadfully at the close, when Baltasar is consumed. He is an admirable soul, as is his beloved seeress Blimunda, but I defer consideration of them until further on, when I can compare their tragic love to other erotic splendors in Saramago. The other visionary center of this turbulent book is the inventive and heretical Padre Bartholomew Lorenzo, an actual personage, who arrived in Portugal from Brazil in 1708. Known to his enemies as "the Flying Man," he invented a bird-like flying machine, called "La passarola," which figures crucially in Saramago's story. I assume Saramago invented the magnificent notion that Domenico Scarlatti himself serenades Baltasar as the one-handed former soldier builds the "Passarola" designed by Padre Lourenço.

It is pure Saramago that the fuel for the flying bird should be provided by Blimunda, who has the unique power to bottle human wills. No surprise here; we are in a romance where the seagulls are "anxious to know if God has aged much." It is however a romance that crosses over into scabrous realism:

> People are saying that the realm is badly governed, and that there is no justice. They fail to understand that this is how the realm ought to be, with its eyes blindfolded and bearing its scales and sword. What more could we wish for, when that is all that has been required: that we should be the weavers of bandages, the inspectors of the weights, the armorers of the sword, constantly mending the holes, adjusting the balance, sharpening the edge of the blade, and then asking the defendant if he is satisfied with the sentence passed on him once he has won or lost his case. We are not referring here to sentences passed by the Holy Office of the Inquisition, which is very astute and prefers an olive branch to scales and a keen blade to one that is jagged and blunt. Some mistake the olive branch as a gesture of peace when it is all too clear that it is kindling wood for the funeral pyre. Either I stab

Contents